To _____

From _____

A 3-minute forever book

EAT YOUR PEAS®

Faithfully,
From Mom

By Cheryl Karpen

Illustrated by Sandy Fougner

At the heart of this little book is a promise.

It's a promise from me to you and it goes like this:

If you ever need someone
to talk to
(really talk to),

someone to hear
(really hear),

what's on your mind and in your heart,

I'll be there for you.

I'm just a phone call, e-mail,
or knock on the door away.

I promise to listen to you

with all my heart.

What's more, I promise to
cherish you,
lift you up and, if I can
help it, never, ever let you down.

In the meantime,
here are a few things
I'd like you
to know,
remember,
and never, ever doubt:

You are a child of God.

Precious and irreplaceable.

You
are the most wonderful
gift
I have ever received.

The first moment I saw you,

I was overwhelmed with joy and wonder.

How could God entrust me with something

so perfect and magnificent?

For the Lord sees every heart
and knows every plan and thought.

1 CHRONICLES 28:9

There are no words to express

a mother's love for her child.

It can only be felt in the heart.

And mine is bursting.

Thank you! Thank you!

THANK YOU God for blessing me

with this extraordinary child.

I have not stopped thanking God for you.
I pray for you constantly.

EPHESIANS 1:16

When God made you,
He made
a one-of-kind
masterpiece.

When I look at you,

I see the beauty of His work.

We are the clay, you are the potter;
And we are all the work of your hand.

ISAIAH 64:8 NIV

There's not another

YOU

in the whole world.

God doesn't do comparisons.

No one has your eyes, your ears, or your little toe.

Made in His image with your own unique set of DNA

means you are way beyond compare!

God
has
blessed
you
with

extraordinary
gifts and talents.

But, wait! You have even more talents

that haven't been revealed to you yet.

Your potential is endless! Each gift will be

revealed with His perfect timing.

He has
a purpose and a plan
for you... and it is good.

Believe.

What plans God has for you!

He created you with a unique purpose in mind.

When your patience feels like it is exhausted

or when life throws you a detour

(and you get really frustrated), be patient. Have faith!

When you surrender your worries and troubles to God,

you will feel a gentle peace inside.

Ask Him for direction and guidance.

He will lead you in the right direction.

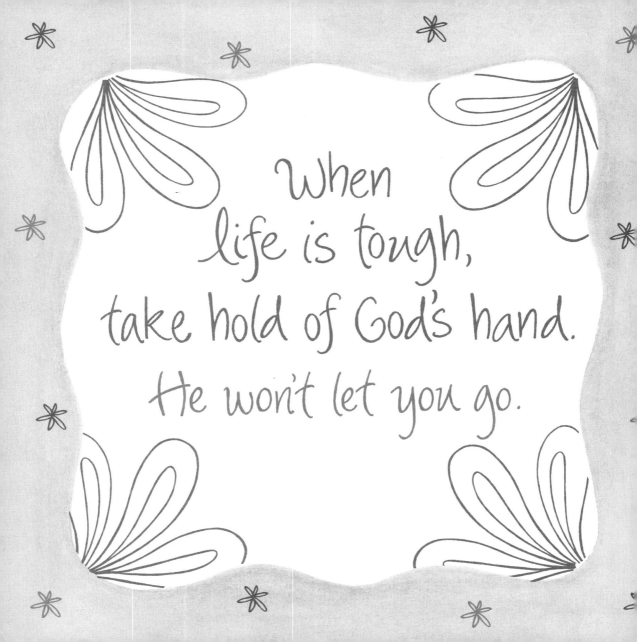

When
life is tough,
take hold of God's hand.
He won't let you go.

Let your faith in Him and His unrelenting faith

in you, lift and carry you through times of uncertainty.

God is always walking beside you.

I am leaving you with a gift—peace of mind and heart.
And the peace I give is a gift the world cannot give.
So don't be troubled or afraid.

JOHN 14:27

Very few burdens
are heavy if we

lift together.

Reaching out to others is a sign

of strength and courage.

So many people love you,

pray for you, and care about you.

Especially me.

Forgiveness
is a
gift.

And
it is
For-giving!

Nothing is as healing and powerful

as the gift of forgiveness, whether it's forgiving

yourself or forgiving others.

Just remember, none of us are perfect.

If God can forgive us for our shortcomings, can't you?

Therefore, my brothers, I want you to know that through
Jesus the forgiveness of sins is proclaimed to you.

ACTS 13:38 NIV

Greet each day
as an opportunity to be
renewed
by
God's love.

Whatever happened yesterday is over.

Let it go and give it up to God.

Embrace each dawn as an opportunity to start anew.

Feel God's love, sweet embrace, and forgiveness.

What do you hope for?

Falling in love, making a scientific
discovery, becoming a missionary, beautifying
the world with your art or words, traveling to the
moon, becoming a father or a mother,
becoming president of the United States?

Keep your hopes and dreams alive.
With God, anything is possible!

Life is a team sport.
Allow God to be
your
#1 coach.

You don't have to do it all on your own.

Through it all, God is there to guide you.

Just remember He has a game plan.

Open your heart and listen.

Seek [the LORD's] will in all you do,
and he will show you which path to take.

PROVERBS 3:6

Nothing is impossible.

You are the hands and feet of God.

Let your imagination and creativity run freely.

(I can hardly wait to see where your

ideas and talents will lead you!)

And it is boundless!

Listen with your heart,

God is calling you to seize your destiny.

Don't be afraid to take chances,

He is your parachute.

Blessed are those who trust in the Lord
and have made the Lord their
hope and confidence.

JEREMIAH 17:7

Obstacles, problems, and roadblocks can
get in the way of your dreams and cause you
to doubt yourself. You will want to quit,
but a voice is whispering in your ear, "Don't
give up." Listen with an open heart. Place your
faith and trust in God. He will give you the
strength and courage to fulfill your purpose.

When doubts filled my mind,
your comfort gave me renewed hope and cheer.

PSALM 94:19

In fact, I'm president of your fan club.

No one asked me to join. I volunteered.

Why are we
on
this
earth?

To give encouragement,

to show kindness,

to extend mercy,

to share love,

to be the warm embrace of Christ.

You shall love your neighbor as yourself.

MATTHEW 19:19

Want to have a
conversation with
the wisest
One
in the world?

Talk to God. Prayer doesn't have to be formal.

He is a good friend who is always there to listen.

Don't worry about anything; instead,
pray about everything. Tell God what you need,
and thank him for all he has done

PHILIPPIANS 4:6

Have faith in His plan.

Although you may not understand some things at the time

(like a broken heart, loss of a dream or a job),

everything really does happen for a reason.

God is all-knowing. Trust in Him.

Be on the lookout for God's surprises.

A smile from a stranger,

a text from a new friend,

an unexpected invitation.

God is calling you to become

closer to Him through others.

The world is full of wonder.

Make the CHOICE to seek peace and happiness.

Be optimistic and focus on the positive.

Others will be attracted to

your joyful spirit.

This is my wish for you:
joy   happiness   peace

contentment   adventure

love   faith   laughter

I pray each day all of
your wishes will come true.

Cell phones, computers,

man on the moon, jet planes,

electricity! Who would have thought any

of these things would be possible?

There is no limit to what you can be and achieve.

I can do everything through Christ,
who gives me strength.

PHILIPPIANS 4:13 NKJV

Wherever you go, whatever you do, I'll always have a

"welcome home"

for you in my heart.

Motherhood doesn't end when your child grows up.

I am here for you even if it's just to listen.

Always listen to your mother.

God even says so!

Though it might not make sense at the time,

I always have your best interests in mind.

I pray to God for guidance so that

I can be the best mom possible.

May the pages of
this little book remind
you of how much
I love and cherish you.

You're one of my
greatest treasures.

Commit everything you do to the LORD.
Trust him and he will help you.
He will make your innocence radiate like the dawn,
and the justice of your cause will shine like the noonday sun.

PSALM 37:5–6

Remember my promise:
I will always be there for you.

To help celebrate your
courage,

to champion your
dreams,

and to remind you to
stay healthy ...

remember to . . .

always
eat your peas!

Why Peas?

She was a vibrant, dazzling young woman with a promising future. Yet, at sixteen, her world felt sad and hopeless.

Though I was living over 1800 miles away, I wanted to let this very special young person in my life know that I would be there for her, across the miles and through the darkness. I wanted her to know she could call me any time, at any hour, and I would be there for her. And I wanted to give her a piece of my heart that she could take with her anywhere—a reminder that she was loved.

Really loved.

Her name is Maddy, and she was the inspiration for my first book in the Eat Your Peas series, *Eat Your Peas for Young Adults.* At the very beginning of her book, I made a place to write in my phone number so she would know I was serious about being available. And right beside the phone number, I put my promise to listen—truly listen—whenever that call came.

Soon after the book was published, people began to ask me if I had the same promise and affirmation for adults. It was then that I realized it isn't just young people who need to be reminded of how truly special they are. We all do.

Today, Maddy is thriving and giving hope to others in her life. I like to think that, in some way, I and my book were part of helping her achieve that. If someone has given you this book, it means *you are a pretty amazing person* to them, and they wanted to let you know. Take it to heart.

Believe it, and remind yourself often.

Wishing you peas and plenty of joy,

Cheryl Karpen

P.S. My mama always said, "Eat your peas! They're good for you." The pages of this book are filled with nutrients for your heart. They're simply good for you too.

A footnote: God works in extraordinary ways. Maddy has grown into one of the most faith-filled and beautiful women I know. She is a gifted wordsmith with a generous and happy heart. Today, ten years after the first Eat Your Peas book was published, Maddy joyfully helped me finish writing the book you now hold in your hands. Together we have come full circle. Thank you, Maddy Dalton, for letting me share your story with the world!

About the author "Eat Your Peas"

A self-proclaimed dreamer, Cheryl
spends her time imagining and creating
between the historic river town of Anoka, Minnesota
and the seaside village of Islamorada, Florida.

An effervescent speaker, Cheryl brings inspiration,
insight, and humor to corporations,
professional organizations, and churches.
Learn more about her at www.cherylkarpen.com

If this book has touched your life,
Cheryl would like to hear your story.
Please send it to mystory@eatyourpeas.com.

About the illustrator

Sandy Fougner artfully weaves
a love for design, illustration and
interiors with being a wife
and mother of three sons.

Other books by Cheryl Karpen

The Eat Your Peas® Collection

now available:

Eat Your Peas® for Mom
Eat Your Peas® Daughter
Eat Your Peas® New Mom
Eat Your Peas® Faithfully

To Let You Know I Care

Eat Your Peas® Faithfully From Mom

Published in Nashville, Tennessee, by Thomas Nelson®.

Thomas Nelson is a trademark of Thomas Nelson, Inc.

Cover design by Koechel Peterson & Associates Minneapolis, MN

ISBN-13: 978-1-4041-8978-2

Printed in China

11 12 13 14 15 [RRD] 5 4 3 2 1

www.thomasnelson.com